Killer Snakes/Serpientes asesinas

# Boa Constrictor/ Boa constrictora

**By Cede Jones**     **Traducción al español: Eduardo Alamán**

**Gareth Stevens**
Publishing

Please visit our Web site, www.garethstevens.com. For a free color catalog of all our high-quality books, call toll free 1-800-542-2595 or fax 1-877-542-2596.

**Cataloging Data**

Jones, Cede.
Boa constrictor/ Boa constrictora
    p. cm. — (Killer snakes / Serpientes asesinas)
Includes bibliographical references and index.
ISBN 978-1-4339-4539-7 (library binding)
1. Boa constrictor—Juvenile literature. I. Title.
QL666.O63J66 2011
597.96'7—dc22

                     2010024475

First Edition

Published in 2011 by
**Gareth Stevens Publishing**
111 East 14th Street, Suite 349
New York, NY 10003

Copyright © 2011 Gareth Stevens Publishing

Designer: Michael J. Flynn
Editor: Greg Roza
Spanish Translation: Eduardo Alamán

Photo credits: Cover, pp. 1, (2–4, 6–8, 10, 12, 14, 16–18, 20–24 snake skin texture), 5, 11, 15, 16–17, 21 Shutterstock.com; pp. 6–7, 13 iStockphoto.com; p. 9 Tim Laman/National Geographic/Getty Images; p. 19 Yuri Cortez/AFP/Getty Images.

Printed in the United States of America

CPSIA compliance information: Batch #CW11GS: For further information contact Gareth Stevens, New York, New York at 1-800-542-2595.

# Contents

- - - - - - - - - - - - - - - - - - - - - - - - - - - - - -

# Contenido

**Boldface** words appear in the glossary/
Las palabras en **negrita** aparecen en el glosario

## Meet the Boa Constrictor

Boa constrictors are large snakes that live in Central and South America. They are good swimmers, but they like to stay on dry land. They can also climb trees. During the day, boa constrictors sleep inside empty trees or holes in the ground. They hunt at night.

-------------------------------

## Conoce a la boa constrictora

Las boa constrictoras son serpientes que viven en Centro y Sur América. Las boas nadan bien, pero también pasan tiempo sobre la tierra. Además, trepan árboles. De día, las boas duermen en árboles vacíos o agujeros en la tierra. De noche salen de cacería.

KEY/CLAVE

boa constrictors/
boas constrictoras

Central America/
América Central

South America/
América del Sur

5

Most adult boa constrictors are between 8 and 10 feet (2.4 and 3 m) long and weigh about 60 pounds (27 kg). However, they can grow up to 13 feet (4 m) long and weigh about 100 pounds (45 kg)! Females are usually larger than males.

-----------------------------------

Las boas constrictoras adultas miden entre 8 y 10 pies (2.4 a 3 m) de largo y pesan unas 60 libras (27 kg). ¡Sin embargo, pueden tener hasta 13 pies (4 m) de largo y pesar hasta 100 libras (45 k)! Las hembras suelen ser más grandes que los machos.

## Made for Hunting

Boa constrictors are made for hunting. They have colors and markings that help them hide. They can be shades of brown, red, green, yellow, and black. Blending into its surroundings allows a boa to surprise its **prey**.

- - - - - - - - - - - - - - - - - - - - - - - - - - - - - -

## Nacidas para cazar

Las boas constrictoras nacen para cazar. Tienen los colores y marcas perfectos para esconderse. Las boas pueden ser de colores marrón, rojo, amarillo y negro. Las boas se esconden para sorprender a su **presas**.

9

The boa constrictor's tongue is like your nose. It can sense odors. By sticking out its tongue, the boa constrictor can "smell" nearby prey. The boa constrictor has special parts around its mouth that sense heat. This helps the boa constrictor find prey in the dark.

---

La lengua de la boa constrictora es como una nariz. La lengua puede detectar olores. Al sacar la lengua, la boa constrictora puede "oler" a sus presas. Además, las boas tienen partes especiales alrededor de la boca que perciben calor. Esto les ayuda a encontrar a sus presas en la oscuridad.

11

## Give Me a Hug

Have you ever been hugged so hard you couldn't breathe? That's what a boa constrictor's hug feels like! Boa constrictors kill prey by wrapping their long bodies around the prey and **squeezing**. This is how they got their name. "Constrict" is another word for "squeeze."

- - - - - - - - - - - - - - - - - - - - - - - - - - - - -

## Abrazos mortales

¿Alguna vez te han abrazado tan fuerte que no puedes respirar? Así es como se siente un abrazo de una boa constrictora. Las boas matan sus presas enredándose en ellas y dándoles un **apretón**. De ahí viene su nombre. "Constricción" es otra palabra para "apretón".

## Let's Eat!

A boa constrictor eats almost anything it can catch, including pigs, lizards, birds, and monkeys. First, it grabs an animal with its teeth. Then, it wraps its body around the animal and squeezes until the prey can't breathe. Some boa constrictors hold an animal underwater until it drowns.

- - - - - - - - - - - - - - - - - - - - - - - - - - - - - - - - -

## ¡A comer!

Las boas constrictoras comen casi todo lo que pueden cazar, incluyendo cerdos, lagartos, aves y monos. Primero, atrapan a sus víctimas con los dientes. Luego enredan su cuerpo alrededor del animal y aprietan hasta que no puede respirar. Algunas boas aprietan a sus víctimas hasta que éstas se ahogan.

14

15

Once a boa constrictor's prey is dead, it's time to eat. A boa constrictor's upper and lower **jaws** can pull apart. This allows the snake to open its mouth really wide. The boa constrictor doesn't chew its food. It swallows the meal whole!

-------------------------------

Una vez que la presa ha muerto, es hora de comer. Las **mandíbulas** de las boas constrictoras se pueden separar. Esto les permite abrir la boca completamente. Las boas no mastican la comida. ¡Las boas se tragan todo el animal!

## Baby Boas

Female boa constrictors give birth to as many as 60 babies at one time. Newborn boa constrictors are between 14 and 22 inches (36 and 56 cm) long. They start hunting right away. Young boa constrictors eat small **rodents**, such as mice and rats.

----

## Bebés de boa

Las constrictoras hembra pueden tener hasta 60 bebés a la vez. Las boas recién nacidas miden entre 14 y 22 pulgadas (36 a 56 cm) de largo. Los bebés comienzan a cazar de inmediato. Las boas jóvenes pueden comer pequeños **roedores** como ratas y ratones.

## Boa Constrictors and People

Many people think boa constrictors attack people, but they don't. Some people keep them as pets! In some places, boa constrictors are valued because they kill pests such as mice and rats. They are sometimes hunted for their skins and for food.

----------------------------------

## Las boas y la gente

Muchas personas creen que las boas atacan a la gente, pero esto no es cierto. ¡Algunas personas las usan como mascotas! En algunos lugares son muy valiosas porque matan pestes como ratas y ratones. Además la gente las caza por su piel y como comida.

# Snake Facts/
# Hoja informativa

## Boa Constrictor/Boa constrictora

| | |
|---|---|
| **Length/Longitud** | usually 8 to 10 feet (2.4 to 3 m) long; up to 13 feet (4 m)<br>entre 8 y 10 pies (2.4 a 3 m) de largo; hasta 13 pies (4 m) |
| **Weight/Peso** | up to 100 pounds (45 kg)<br>hasta 100 libras (45 kg) |
| **Where It Lives/ Hábitat** | Central and South America<br>América Central y América del Sur |
| **Life Span/ Años de vida** | 20 to 30 years<br>de 20 a 30 años |
| **Killer Fact/ Método de matar** | Boa constrictors have hooked teeth. They curve backwards! This helps boas hold onto their prey while wrapping their bodies around the meal.<br>Las boas constrictoras tienen dientes de gancho. Esto les ayuda a sujetar a sus víctimas mientras las atrapan con sus cuerpos. |

# Glossary/Glosario

**jaw:** the upper or lower part of the mouth

**prey:** an animal caught and eaten by another animal

**rodent:** a small, furry animal with large front teeth, such as a mouse

**squeeze:** to press something tightly

- - - - - - - - - - - - - - - - - - - - - - - - - - - - - - - -

**apretón (el)** apretar algo muy fuerte

**mandíbula (la)** Las partes superiores e inferiores de la boca

**presa (la)** un animal que es atrapado por otro para comer

**roedores (los)** pequeños animales peludos con largos dientes, como los ratones

# For More Information/Más información

## Books/Libros

Gunderson, Megan M. *Boa Constrictors.* Edina, MN: ABDO Publishing, 2011.

Sexton, Colleen. *Boa Constrictors.* Minneapolis, MN: Bellwether Media, 2010.

## Web Sites/Páginas en Internet

### Boa Constrictors

*kids.nationalgeographic.co.in/kids/animals/creaturefeature/boa/*
Read more about boa constrictors and see photos of the snake.

### Reptiles: Boa

*www.sandiegozoo.org/animalbytes/t-boa.html*
Read about the differences between boas, pythons, and anacondas.

# Index/Índice